C000000915

Improve Your Sight-singing!

ELEMENTARY LEVEL

Paul Harris & Mike Brewer

© 1997 by Faber Music Ltd
First published in 1997 by Faber Music Ltd
3 Queen Square London WC1N 3AU
Music and text set by Wessex Music Services
Cover design by S & M Tucker
Printed in England by Halstan & Co Ltd

ISBN 0 571 51767 6

ff

FABER
MUSIC

INTRODUCTION

Whether you are a member of a choir, a singer or instrumentalist preparing for the sight-singing tests in grade exams or simply enjoy singing with friends, the ability to sight-sing with confidence and accuracy is a most important musical skill.

Using the workbook

Improve Your Sight-singing! offers a progressive series of enjoyable and stimulating stages which, if you use them systematically, will rapidly improve your reading ability. You can either work through the book on your own at home, with a friend (perhaps a fellow member of your choir) or, if you have a teacher, during your lessons.

After the preliminary stage, **Awakening your ear**, each stage consists of two parts: firstly, specially-written, original exercises and pieces which you should take time to prepare (pp.5-30); and secondly, unprepared tests, which include pieces by well-known composers (pp.31-40).

At the top of the first page in each stage are the new features being introduced. At the end of the stage, should you want to monitor your progress, there is an assessment box.

There are four different types of exercise:

Rhythmic exercises   It is very important that you feel and maintain a steady pulse: these exercises will help develop this ability. There are at least four ways of doing them: clap or tap the lower line (the beat or pulse) while singing the upper line to 'la' (or any other syllable); tap the lower line with your foot and clap the upper line; on a table or flat surface, tap the lower line with one hand and the upper line with the other; 'play' the lower line on a metronome and clap or tap the upper line.

Melodic exercises   Once you are confident you have grasped the particular rhythmic pattern you can then focus on the melodic exercises. Fluent sight-singing is greatly improved by the ability to 'pre-hear' intervals and to recognise melodic shapes at a glance. These shapes are often related to scale and arpeggio patterns, so before you sing each exercise look through it first and see whether there are any recognisable patterns which will make your singing more fluent.

Prepared pieces   Take time to ask yourself the questions which apply to the vocal line and appear before some of the pieces, and devise more of these questions yourself. Prepare these pieces carefully as they will give you practice at many rhythmic and melodic patterns you will encounter time after time. The first exercise can be accompanied by an optional second voice singing the lower part but using the same words (perhaps your teacher or a friend) or you could play the lower line on the piano. Exercises 2 and 3 have simple (optional) piano accompaniments. Try to get a friend (or your teacher) to play them if possible – they will help you to develop the musical ideas and help you to sing in tune. You could play them yourself or, if your pianistic skills are modest, just try adding the left hand or bass line only.

Unprepared pieces   Finally, when you are confident you can sing all the work in the stage with real security, try the unprepared tests which you should read without preparation – at sight.

Some helpful suggestions have been made throughout the book but these need not be strictly adhered to. There are also references to useful tunes to help you remember intervals.

The authors wish to thank Debbie Lammin for many helpful suggestions.

PRELIMINARY STAGE

Counting

If you have a metronome, start it clicking at ♩ = 60 (if you haven't, find a clock with a loud tick). What you're hearing is a beat or pulse, and you must learn to feel this whenever you sing. A good sight-singer has a kind of inner metronome clicking away, helping to keep the music steady and the rhythm in time.

Here are some exercises to help you develop your ability to count:

1 Clap or tap the top line and count the beat **out loud**.

2 Now repeat exercise 1 counting in your head.

Clap or tap the next exercises – first counting out loud, then in your head.

3

4
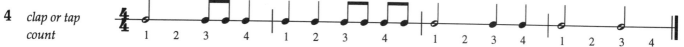

Awakening your ear

Perhaps the most important skill you need to develop is the ability to **listen**, both to pitch and to sound colour. You may find the following exercises and games very helpful – come back to them from time to time.

Find the note G on an instrument and then the E below it. Sing them to 'ma'.

These two notes form an almost universal pattern – the characteristic 'chant' sung by children all over the world:

Using these notes have a simple conversation in song with yourself, a friend or your teacher. For example:

How are you?__ I've got a head-ache. Take some as-p'rin. Thank you ve-ry much.__

Now play the notes on an instrument to check your pitch hasn't changed.

Now add the note A above G. Make up phrases using vowel sounds (to produce a smooth legato) e.g.

la _____   ma _____

When singing phrases such as these, try to 'hear' the next note in your head before you sing it.

Now add the notes D and C:

You can now sing a pentatonic scale:

With a friend or your teacher, each sing these notes in a random order, to any rhythm, pausing occasionally. Whatever you sing, the duet will sound effective!

Now add the note F. Begin with descending patterns, then explore all six notes, singing them to 'ma':

Now you can play games with these notes. Sing them in any combination, perhaps getting a friend or your teacher to suggest the pattern. Use numbers or note names or sol-fa, e.g.

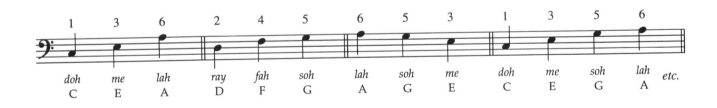

Stage 1

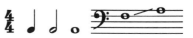

Tones in F major, using notes 1 - 3 of the scale.

Rhythmic exercises

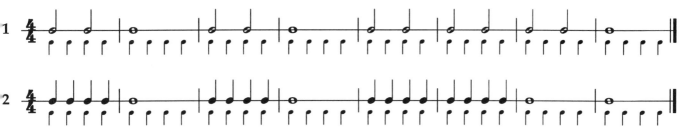

Melodic exercises

Sing the next exercises in any or all of the following ways:

- to the scale number (ie 1, 2, 3, 2 *etc.*)
- to the note name (ie F, G, A, G *etc.*)
- to 'ma' (remember to keep the front of your tongue down behind your lower teeth)
- to tonic sol-fa

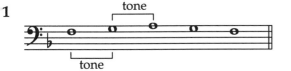

Now clap the following rhythms (A, B and C); then clap the rhythms as you sing the exercises:

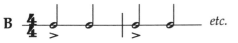

Sing the next two exercises to 'ma' whilst clapping the pulse; then sing them to the scale number or note name.

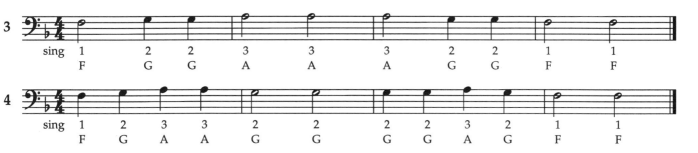

5   At this stage you might like to *say* the words to the rhythms before
    singing them (or you can sing the following exercises to 'ma', or
    another syllable if you prefer).

Let   there   be   light: and   there   was   light.

Was your F in the final bar exactly the same pitch as the first note?

Prepared pieces

Words: Anon.

1

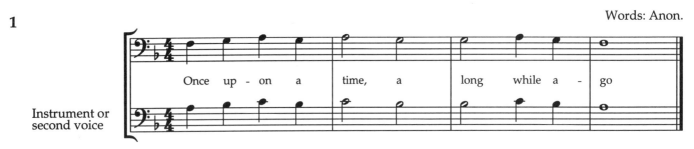

Instrument or
second voice

Once up - on a   time, a   long while a - go

Make sure you or your teacher plays the key chord before you start the
piece. Follow and listen to the piano introduction for each piece as it
will help you to *pre-hear* your first note.

2   In which key is this song? Play and sing your starting note.
    Sing the interval between F and G/G and A. What are these intervals?

Words: Alexander Lyell

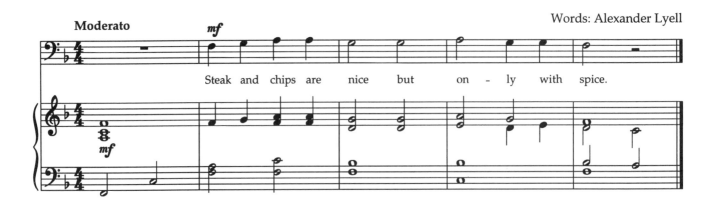

Moderato   *mf*

Steak and chips are   nice but   on - ly   with   spice.

3 Play and sing your starting note.
How many beats in the bar will you count?

Moderato

mf

Words: William Blake

Ti - ger! Ti - ger! Burn -ing bright   in   the fo - rests of   the night.

Each stage of the book has its own unprepared pieces, beginning on
Page 31 for Stage 1.

Self/teacher's assessment

Satisfactory	
Good	
Excellent	

Useful tunes:
The following tunes begin with three tones:
Ascending: Frère Jacques
Descending: Three blind mice

Unprepared pieces: page 31

Stage 2

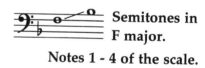

**Semitones in
F major.**

Notes 1 - 4 of the scale.

Rhythmic exercises

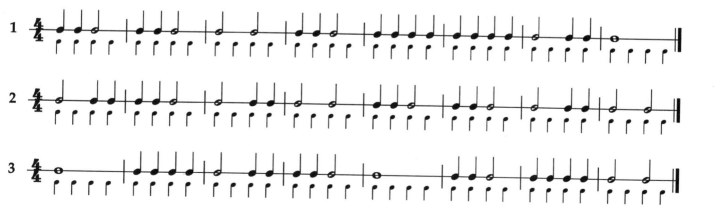

8

Melodic exercises

Practise the following exercises in the same way as Stage 1. Add the
syllable 'na' (don't forget to bring your tongue down close behind your
lower teeth for the vowel).

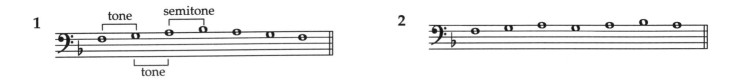

Look carefully at the melodic shapes in the next three exercises.
What patterns do you notice?

Don't forget to *say* the words to the rhythms before singing them.

Words: William Shakespeare

Prepared pieces

Words: Anon.

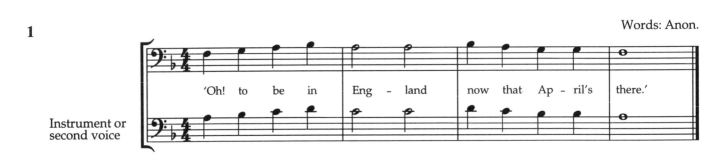

2 In which key is this song?
How will you find your first note?

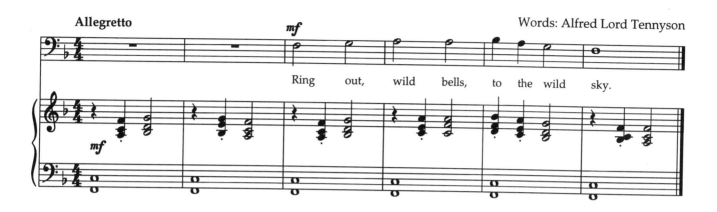

Allegretto

mf

Words: Alfred Lord Tennyson

Ring out, wild bells, to the wild sky.

mf

3 Compare the melodic shape of the phrases (bars 2-3 and 4-5).
What do they have in common?

Moderato

mf

Words: Anon.

Rail-road Bill lived up the hill, ne - ver worked and ne - ver will.

mf

Self/teacher's assessment

Satisfactory	
Good	
Excellent	

Unprepared pieces: page 32

Stage 3

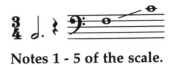

Notes 1 - 5 of the scale.

Rhythmic exercises

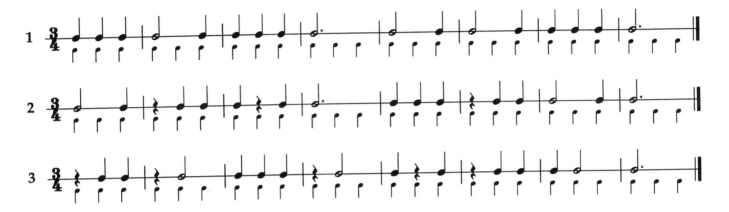

Melodic exercises

Practise the following exercises in the same way as Stage 1. Add the
syllable 'doo'.

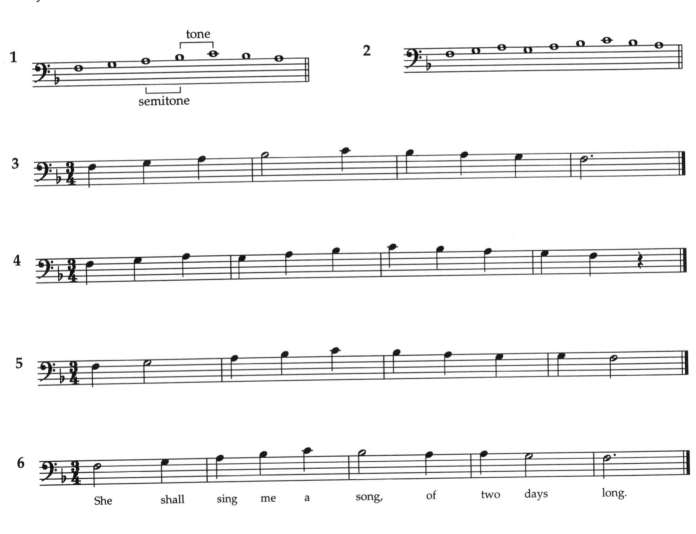

She   shall   sing   me   a   song,   of   two   days   long.

Prepared pieces

1

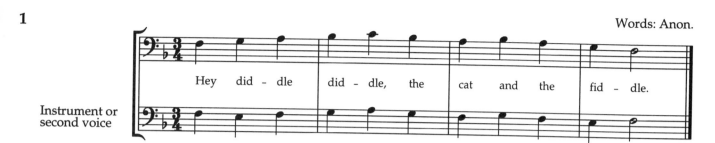

Words: Anon.

Instrument or second voice

Hey did – dle did – dle, the cat and the fid – dle.

2 In which key is this song? Play the key chord.
How will you find your first note?

Andante espressivo

mp

Words: Robert Louis Stevenson

Home is the sai – lor, home from the sea, And the hun – ter home from the hill.

mp sim.

Con ped.

3 Play the key chord.
How will you give character to this song?

Allegro

f

Words: Anon.

Jack and Jill went up the hill to fetch a pail of wa – ter.

f

Self/teacher's assessment

Satisfactory	
Good	
Excellent	

Unprepared pieces: page 33

Stage 4

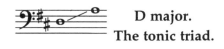

D major.
The tonic triad.

Rhythmic exercises

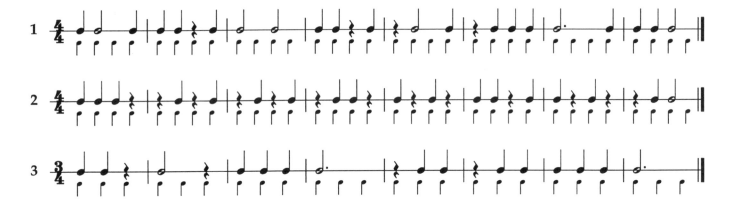

Melodic exercises

Add the syllable 'la'. Enjoy the sensation of singing the consonant 'l'.
Let the tongue fall naturally for the vowel and keep your jaw relaxed.

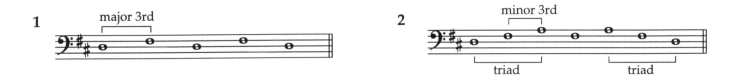

5 What particular melodic patterns do you see in the first bar of the next
two exercises?

7

8

Words: Anon.

The boy stood on the burn - ing deck, his fleece was white as snow.

Prepared pieces

Look through the next three pieces making a mental note of where the tonic triads occur.

1

Words: John Keats

There was a naugh-ty boy, a naugh-ty boy was he.

Instrument or second voice

2 In which key is this song? Play and sing up the notes of the triad.
What pattern is formed by the first five notes?

Allegro giocoso f

Words: Anon.

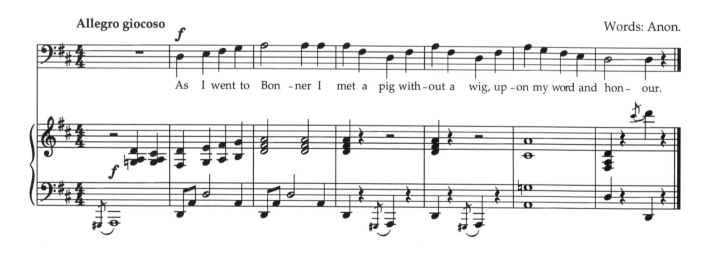

As I went to Bon -ner I met a pig with-out a wig, up -on my word and hon- our.

3 What melodic pattern is formed by the first three notes?
Compare bars 2, 3 and 5.

Words: Anon.

I saw a wasp up-on the wall and did not like his face at all!

Self/teacher's assessment

Satisfactory	
Good	
Excellent	

Useful tunes:
The following tunes begin with a major third:
Ascending: While shepherds watched their flocks by night
O when the saints
Descending: Beethoven's 5th Symphony (First movement)
Swing low, sweet chariot

Unprepared pieces: page 34

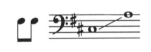

The leading note
(7th note of scale) in
D major. Notes 7
and 1 - 5 of the scale.

Stage 5

Rhythmic exercises

Melodic exercises

Practise with any of the syllables you've learned already, or any other
nonsense syllable of your choice. You can improve your singing whilst
sight-reading by using a mixture of vowels and resonating consonants,
eg. 'zee', 'va', 'ba' and so on. Don't forget to use scale numbers and
note names (or sol-fa) too.

Here are some new rhythmic patterns to clap as you sing (once you can
sing the notes with confidence!)

Make a mental note of which notes are affected by the key signature in
the next four pieces. Now find the semitone intervals (you may like to
mark them with a bracket).

What melodic pattern is the following exercise based on?

Words: Edward Lear

The Owl and the Pus-sy cat went to sea in a beau-ti-ful pea-green boat.

* Sing these intervals; what intervals are they?

Prepared pieces

1

Words: Anon.

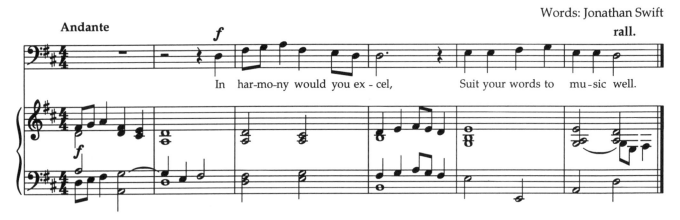

We're all in the dumps, for di-a-monds are trumps. The kit-tens are gone to St. Paul's.

Instrument or second voice

2 In which key is this song? Play and sing up the notes of the triad.
How will you find your first note?
How will the piano introduction help you?

Words: Jonathan Swift

Andante *f* **rall.**

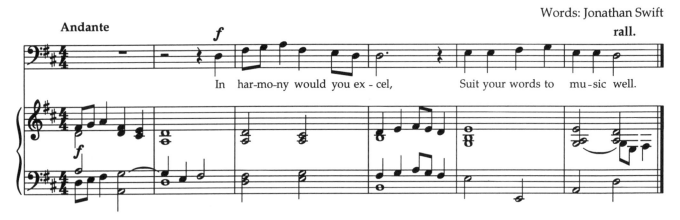

In har-mo-ny would you ex - cel,   Suit your words to   mu -sic well.

3 Play and sing up the notes of the triad.
How will you find your first note?
What is the technical name for the C sharps in bars 4 and 5?

Words: Anon.

Allegretto *mf*

The man in the moon came tum-bling down And ask'd his way to   Nor - wich.

Self/teacher's assessment

Satisfactory	
Good	
Excellent	

Useful tunes:
The following tunes begin with a minor third:
Ascending: Greensleeves
Descending: Song of the Volga Boatmen
                 Children's chant (see page 3)

Unprepared pieces: page 35

Stage 6

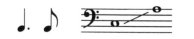

Rhythmic exercises

1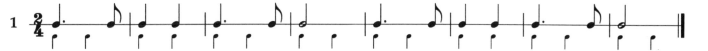

2

3

Melodic exercises

1 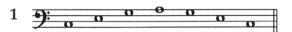   2

3

4

5

6

7

Words: William Shakespeare

When shall we three meet a - gain, in thun - der, light - ning or in rain?

Prepared pieces

1

Words: Thomas Hood

I re - mem - ber, I re - mem - ber the house where I was born.

Instrument or second voice

2 In which key is this song? Play and sing up the notes of the triad.
How will you find your first note?
What melodic pattern is formed by the first four notes?

Words: Algernon Swinburne

One, who is not, we see; but one whom we see not, is.

3 Play and sing up the notes of the triad.
How will you find your first note?
What does **Allegro giocoso** mean?
How will you communicate the character of this song?

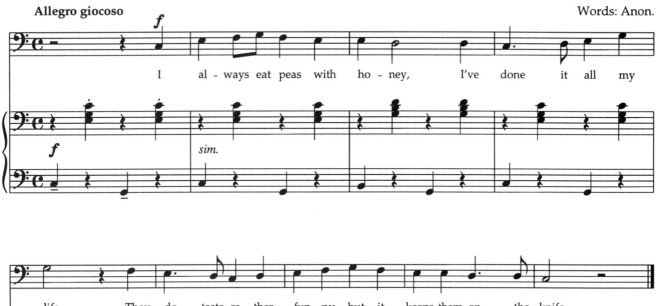

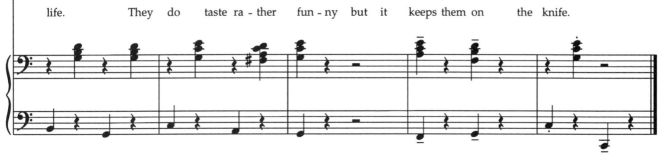

Self/teacher's assessment

Satisfactory	
Good	
Excellent	

Useful tunes:
The following tunes begin with a major triad:
Ascending: The Blue Danube
Descending: Jesus Christ Superstar

Unprepared pieces: page 36

Stage 7

More notes below the tonic in F and D major. More than one note to a syllable.

Rhythmic exercises

1

2

3

Melodic exercises

1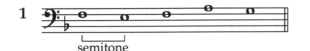

2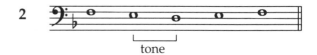

3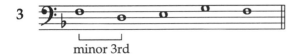

4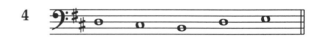

5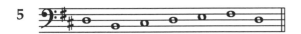

6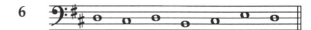

7

8

9

10

Words: Anon.

A hap – py man walk'd up and down, to buy his din – ner in the town.

Was your F in the final bar exactly the same pitch as the first note?

Prepared pieces

Work out where the semitone intervals are in the next three pieces.

1

Words: Laurence Sterne

I saw, I saw I know not what, I saw a dash a – bove a dot.

Instrument or second voice

2 In which key is this song? Play and sing up the notes of the triad.
On what melodic pattern are the first four notes based?
What is the interval between the F and D in bar 3?
Beginning on any note, sing that interval descending.

Ye sac – red mu – ses Race of Jove, Whom mu – sic's love de – light – eth.

3 In which key is this song? Play and sing up the notes of the triad.
What is the interval between the second and third notes?
Sing this interval.
What is the interval between the final two notes? Sing this interval.

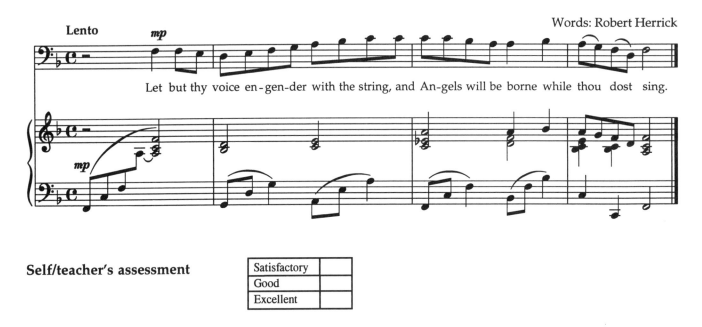

Words: Robert Herrick

Self/teacher's assessment

Satisfactory	
Good	
Excellent	

Unprepared pieces: page 37

Stage 8

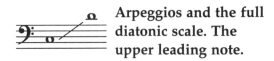

Arpeggios and the full
diatonic scale. The
upper leading note.

Rhythmic exercises

Melodic exercises

I come from the ci - ty of Bos - ton, the home of the bean and the cod.

Prepared pieces

1

Words: Anon.

I ask'd the maid in dul - cet tone to or - der me a but - tered scone.

Instrument or second voice

2 In which key is the song? Play and sing up the notes of the triad.
On which degree of the scale does this song begin?
What is the interval between the second and third notes?
Sing this interval.

Allegro

Words: Anon.

f

Poor Mar-tha Snell, she's gone a-way. She would if she could, but she could-n't stay.

3 In which key is this song? Play and sing up the notes of the triad.
Compare the rhythm of bar 8 with bars 3-7.
How will you find your first note?

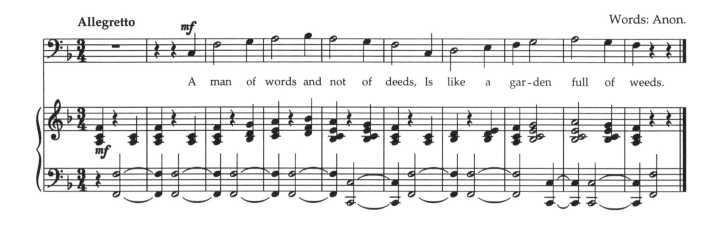

Allegretto

mf

Words: Anon.

A man of words and not of deeds, Is like a gar-den full of weeds.

Self/teacher's assessment

Satisfactory	
Good	
Excellent	

Unprepared pieces: page 38

Stage 9

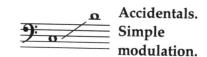 **Accidentals. Simple modulation.**

Rhythmic exercises

Melodic exercises

Remember that accidentals affect the pitch of a note for the whole bar, unless corrected. Make up your own endings to the following exercises:

continue

continue

6

The Pob - ble who has no toes, had once as ma - ny as we. *continue using the text below*

When they said 'Some day you may lose them all,' He replied, - 'Fish fiddle de-dee!'

Prepared pieces

1

Words: John Gay

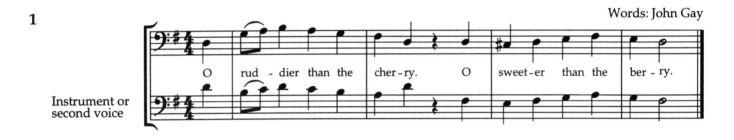

O rud - dier than the cher - ry. O sweet - er than the ber - ry.

Instrument or second voice

2 How will you give character to this song?
In which key is it? Play and sing up the notes of the triad.
The key changes (or modulates) in this song. In which key does it end?

Allegro maestoso

Glo - ri - a, Glo - ri - a in ex - cel - sis De - o.

3 In which key does this song begin? and end?
What is the interval between the E and F sharp (bar 3/4)?
Sing this interval.
Compare the rhythm of the two phrases (bars 1-5 and bars 5-9)

Words: Henry Vaughan

My soul there is a coun - try far be - yond the stars. Where stands a wing - ed sen - try all skil - ful in the wars.

Self/teacher's assessment

Satisfactory	
Good	
Excellent	

Useful tunes:
The following tunes begin with a fourth:
Ascending: London's burning
Descending: Eine kleine Nachtmusik

Unprepared pieces: page 39

Stage 10

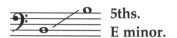

5ths.
E minor.

Rhythmic exercises

Melodic exercises

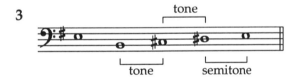

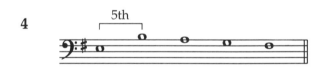

7

8

Words: Robert Burns

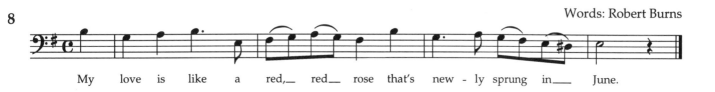

My love is like a red,— red— rose that's new - ly sprung in— June.

Prepared pieces

1

Words: George Herbert

My heart leaps up when I— be - hold a rain - bow in— the sky.

Instrument or
second voice

2 In which key is this song? Play and sing up the notes of the triad.
What differences can you spot between the two phrases (marked by a
bracket)?

Allegretto con moto

Words: Lewis Carroll

mf

'Will you walk a lit - tle fast - er?' said a whi - ting to a snail, 'There's a

mf

por - poise close be - hind us, and he's tread - ing on my tail.'

3 Identify the two phrases. What are their differences and similarities?
Play and sing up the notes of the triad.

Words: William Shakespeare

O Mis-tress mine, where are you roam-ing? O! stay and hear; your true love's com-ing.

Self/teacher's assessment

Satisfactory	
Good	
Excellent	

Useful tunes:
The following tunes begin with a fifth:
Ascending: Twinkle, twinkle little star
Descending: But who may abide? (Messiah)

Unprepared pieces: page 40

Unprepared Pieces - Stage 1

Exercises 1, 2 and 3 may be sung to any of the syllables introduced so far, scale numbers, note names, sol-fa or any other syllable.

Stage 2

1    **2**

3

4

Thomas Ravenscroft

Ro - bin Hood,   Ro - bin Hood, said   Lit - tle   John, come dance be - fore the   Queen.

5 Moderato

Heinrich Schütz

mf

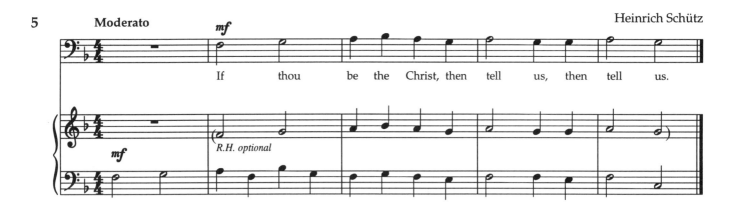

If   thou   be the Christ, then tell   us, then tell   us.

R.H. optional

mf

Stage 3

Stage 4

Stage 5

Henry Purcell

Since time so kind to us does prove, so kind to us does prove.

Moderato

Heinrich Schütz

Need we a - ny fur - ther wit - ness? Need we a - ny fur - ther

wit - ness? For we our - selves have heard it out of his own mouth.

Stage 6

Franz Schubert

The grave is deep and sound - less and ter - ri - ble its face, its

black - est depth is bound - less, an un - dis - co - vered place.

Allegro maestoso

Carl Maria von Weber (adapted)

Glo - ri - a, Glo - ri - a in ex - cel - sis De - o,

Glo - ri - a, Glo - ri - a in ex - cel - sis De - o.

Stage 7

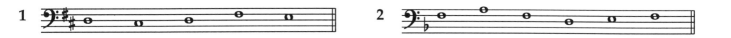

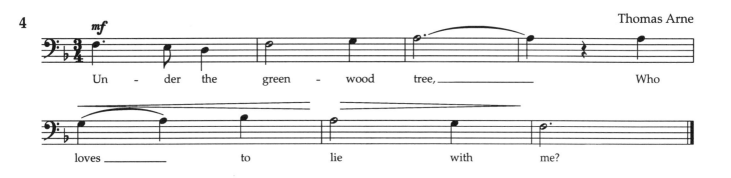

Stage 8

1

3

4

Jonathan Battishill

Here on his back doth lay Sir An - drew Keel - ing, Sir An - drew Keel - ing.

5 Allegro

Traditional

A jol - ly fat— frog— lived in the ri - ver swim O! A come - ly black— crow— lived on the ri - ver brim O!

Stage 9

Stage 10

Johannes Brahms

And if ____ you go to the church - - yard the church - - - yard, a new - ly filled grave ____ you'll find, you'll find.

Henry Purcell

Crown the al - - tar, deck ____ the shrine,

Crown the al - - tar, ____ deck ____ the ____ shrine, ____ the shrine.